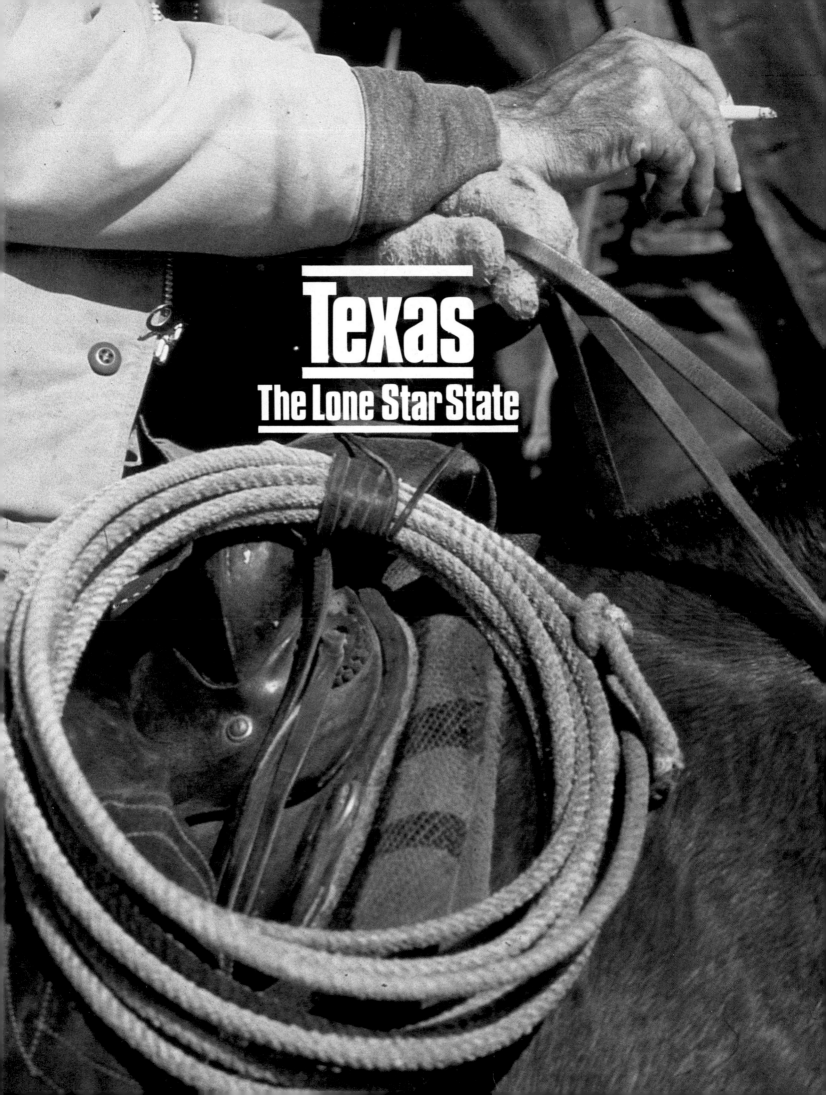

Texas
The Lone Star State

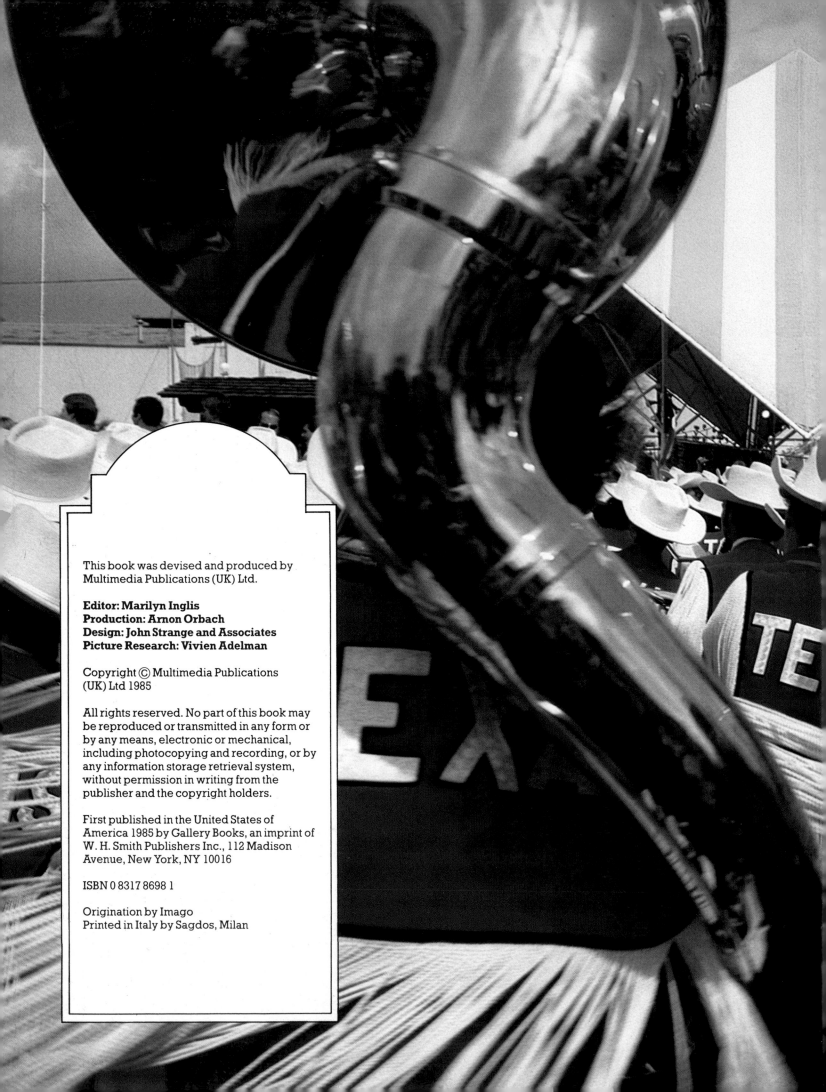

This book was devised and produced by
Multimedia Publications (UK) Ltd.

Editor: Marilyn Inglis
Production: Arnon Orbach
Design: John Strange and Associates
Picture Research: Vivien Adelman

First published in the United States of
America 1985 by Gallery Books, an imprint of
W. H. Smith Publishers Inc., 112 Madison
Avenue, New York, NY 10016

ISBN 0 8317 8698 1

Origination by Imago
Printed in Italy by Sagdos, Milan

Texas
The Lone Star State
Carole Chester

GALLERY BOOKS
An Imprint of W. H. Smith Publishers Inc.
112 Madison Avenue
New York City 10016

CONTENTS

CHAPTER 1

The Lone Star State

"The Lone Star State" … "The Big T" … Texas! It's cowboy country from way back, though these days anyone can ride tall in the saddle at a Texas ranch and listen to a moody melody at a cookout. These days, too, they can shoot for the stars — literally — for the state's Space Age cities are known for their astronauts.

Texas is so vast — bigger than France, Switzerland, Belgium, the Netherlands and Luxembourg put together — it's not surprising it didn't want any part of the Union. Indeed, it was independent between 1836 and 1845. Its size has given it its contrasts, changeable scenery and climate — and its pride.

In this magnificent state there are plains and prairies, mountains and rivers, deserts and palm trees. The land's very enormity may account for the largesse of the Texans themselves — hospitable and eager to welcome visitors to view their riches. The name "Texas" actually comes from an Indian word "tejas", meaning "friends", and though the locals may at times seem a little overpowering, in truth it's just goodheartedness.

Many songs have been written about Texas and its oil power has made it the setting for one of television's most popular "soaps". One can feel the power — of earth and sunlight, of industry and entrepreneurs. The rawness of new power coupled with the brashness inherited from the original pioneers. The gleaming image presented by look-at-me cities like Houston, so grown up, so fast.

But there's a softness, too; where waves lap gently against the Gulf Islands and the tinkling of mariachi music can be heard in towns where eyes are remarkably Spanish.

There are some 50 state parks, two national parks, a national seashore and four national forests. There are 90 or so peaks that tower more than a mile high, over 600 miles of beach and 4500 square miles of inland lakes and streams. Impressive indeed. There's far more to Texas than oil.

Central Texas is fishing and boating country, and boasts the state capital, Austin, too. Southern Texas encompasses both mellowed old Spanish missions and the NASA Space Center. Western Texas is range country and once challenged the wagon train pioneers. East Texas has a southern spirit about it, with antebellum houses and moss-draped trees.

Oil was first discovered in 1894, but until it started gushing at Spindletop in 1901, agriculture and cattle-raising were the basis of the Texas economy. Once "black gold" erupted, related industries began to spring up and Texas took on a new face. It now leads the nation in the production of petroleum and natural gas.

Not all of its cities are as famous as Dallas/Forth Worth, Houston or even San Antonio, yet somehow their names ring a familiar bell. Corpus Christi, an international seaport where the Padre Island National Seashore begins. Brownsville, largest city in the Rio Grande Valley. Laredo, major cross-through point for the highway down to Mexico City. Lubbock, rich in cotton. Abilene with its wild, wild past.

Put on a stetson and we'll tour Texas!

Facing page above In this general store at Luckenbach on the Pecos Trail time seems to have stood still. Although you may imagine for a moment you are back in the Wild West, today the Trans-Pecos is well known for its oil production.

Facing page below Here at the Ranching Heritage Center in Lubbock there is a museum with around 30 different examples of ranches brought from all over the state to illustrate the history of ranching in Texas, plus these reconstructed store fronts.

Left This young Indian is proudly displaying that the culture and heritage of his people is not lost.

Above This fine specimen of the cow-tongue prickly-pear demonstrates clearly how it came by its name.

Above Apart from its historic trades, Texas is a thriving, bustling modern state where new buildings are constantly in progress.

Right The activities of the oil industry are unceasing. Here, roughnecks are making up a drill pipe with tongs and pipe spinner.

Above Although the Texan lifestyle is in large part based on oil, Texans do not believe in taking it too seriously, as these nodding donkeys show.

Left The public image of the oil industry is inextricably linked with furs, jewels and soap operas; but the reality is jobs and wages on a smaller scale for thousands, as well.

Facing page The Texas State Capitol Building in Austin is open to tourists every day and must surely be voted a favorite for sightseers. It dates from 1888, and is seven feet higher than the US Capitol.

Above Something sure is engrossing these Texans. It's hard to concentrate on your food when a cowboy is about to part from his mount at a rodeo!

Left In the State Office Building you can see the Six Flags of Texas, commemorating the days when Texas was under Spain, France, Mexico, when it was a Republic, when it was part of the Confederacy, and now as a state in the United States.

Below Only in Texas would you find a car ranch. Here at the Cadillac Ranch at Amarillo, ten Cadillacs present their tail fins to the sky, representing each style from 1949 to 1963.

Bottom Texas has a wide range of sports to offer. If the dust, heat and noise of a rodeo is not to your taste, perhaps some marlin fishing will fit the bill.

Above left You haven't really visited Texas if you don't sample a rodeo, where all the old skills of the cowboy are demonstrated. You'll find both large and small ones all over the state – and even a Prison Rodeo in Huntsville, where the inmates take part!

Left The Saturn V was launched for the first time on November 9, 1967. The noise of its launching was such that the roof of the Columbia Broadcasting System's television booth collapsed, three miles away. Here, at NASA, you can examine at close quarters this example of man's ingenuity.

CHAPTER 2

Yesterday's Texas

Texas knew six flags before it became the 28th state of America. Spain was the first nation to claim it, from 1519 to 1685 and again from 1719 to 1821. Those legendary conquistadors and the missionaries worked among the Indians to build a chain of missions and bring harmony to this land.

From 1685 to 1690, France claimed this new territory after explorer-nobleman, Sieur de La Salle, landed here. Robert Cavalier founded the colony of Fort St Louis near Navasota but it didn't survive for long. He was murdered and there were just a handful of inhabitants when the colony was re-established by the Spanish some four years later.

The intermingling of cultures happened under the tricolor flag of Mexico. Old Spain's adventures vied with newcomers from the US. Though the 1836 declaration of independence declared Texas to be free politically, the Latin influences remained.

Texas was an independent republic from 1836 to 1845 — a colorful era for those who were footloose, fancy free and quick on the draw. When the Civil War broke out, Texas sided with the Confederacy. Though the ensuing war brought devastation to much of the South, at the end of it, Texas discovered it had potential — in the form of its longhorns.

These cattle provided the beef that the growing nation needed. And then came the oil. Texas, as part of the United States between 1845 and 1861, and again in 1865, prospered.

Yesterday's small trading posts have grown into today's cities. John Neely Bryan founded Dallas in 1841 as one such trading post, on the banks of the Trinity River. "Cowtown" Fort Worth was put on the economic map thanks to post-Civil War cattle drives up the Chisholm Trail.

Many early settlers made their homes in the vicinity of Austin in central Texas — a

rich, fertile area. They built haciendas, and later in the eighteenth century, there were German colonial mansions here. (During President Johnson's reign, "The Little White House" — the LBJ Ranch — was located on the Pedernales River, southwest of town.)

Rich Texas as we know it began with the gushing at Spindletop in the twentieth century. From Port Arthur, with its immense refineries and oil storage facilities, you can drive to the edge of the Gulf of Mexico, to Port Bolivar. Here, ferries make their way to Galveston, an island city founded by pirate Jean Lafitte in 1817. Tragically, this city lost thousands of citizens in the great flood and hurricane of 1900.

Above left A fine example of the Texas longhorn, around which so much of the state's history has been built.

Above right Ranch signs are an art in themselves, their vivid images standing out boldly above the ranch entrances.

Right These two cowboys are just as likely nowadays to be working from a truck or even a plane. But there is some terrain for which a horse is still best.

No matter where you go in Texas, there's no escape from history. From Laredo, for instance, it's a "Wild West" drive to San Antonio. It was west Texas that daunted the pioneers, though it's easily crossed today. The area around Del Rio is sheep country. It was here that Judge Roy Bean, a law unto himself, held court in his saloon, named for his idol Lillie Langtry — for whom he also named his town. He's buried in the grounds of the Whitehead Memorial Museum.

The tough longhorns that roamed the Texas Panhandle have been replaced by more modern breeds of cattle. Cowboys still ride the vast plains, though they may be in helicopters or jeeps as much as in the saddle. The Permian Basin, a flat prairie that

Above Branding your cattle is just as important as it always was – and rustling is just as unpopular today with the cattle barons as it was in the past.

Left These could almost be hieroglyphs on an ancient Egyptian monument – but in fact they are the cattle brands of Texan ranches.

was once an ancient sea, boasts a valuable oil treasury. Midland, one of two cities here, was a rich farming community in the 1870s, taking its name from its location — midway between Fort Worth and El Paso. The Comanche War Trail went through here, later becoming the Chihuahua Trail for California-bound pioneers. Oil was discovered in 1923 and now Midland is a big oil town.

Many Texan cities were named for prominent people of their times. Henry W. Karnes, a Texas revolutionary figure and Indian fighter, gave his name to Karnes City. The German Prince Carl of Braunfels founded New Braunfels in 1845 — this growing city still retains its German heritage and small town charm.

Juan N. Seguin was a respected Tex-Mexican who served in Sam Houston's army. The town founded as Walnut Springs was renamed Seguin in his honor in 1839. Crockett was named for the famous Davy by a man who served with him in Sam Houston's army. Other towns were named for forts: Fort Stockton, for example, where a cavalry post was established in 1859 to guard the wagon trains and stagecoaches. Like other west Texas cities, San Angelo,

too, owes its existence to a fort — Fort Concho, established in 1867 as an outpost in hostile Indian country. And Gatesville grew from the 1849 protective fort.

In yesterday's Texas, water was as magical as oil is today. The "Big Spring", for which today's city was named, was an oasis for those who rode the wagon trains and also for the Indians. It was later used by cattle barons passing through the area. The world's first-ever rodeo is said to have been held in rough tough Pecos in 1883. This town's West-of-the-Pecos Museum occupies the saloon in what used to be the area's finest hotel! And one of the old town graves is that of "Gentleman Gunfighter" Clay Allison. (Many towns have found fame thanks to their gun-toting days. Round Rock, in the ranch and hill country, is the place where notorious outlaw Sam Bass was killed. His gang plagued many a stagecoach, train and bank.)

Not surprisingly, many Texas communities were originally Indian settlements. Nacogdoches is one which claims to be Texas' oldest town. Huntsville was founded as an Indian trading post in 1836 though Sam Houston was one of its early prominent residents. The Spanish

Below The Lyndon Baines Johnson National Historic Park and State Park have everything to offer the visitor – wildlife reserves, tennis, swimming, a historic farm – and, of course, the birthplace, ranch and grave of the only US president to come from Texas.

padres helped introduce agriculture which, until the oil boom, was a major part of the Texas economy. The orange grove planted by the Oblate Fathers in 1824, three miles south of what is today called Mission, is said to be one of the first experiments with citrus culture in the lower Rio Grande Valley. Perhaps this is one reason why the town today presents itself as "Home of the Grapefruit" — the Texas Ruby Red variety.

Yesterday's Texas is one of lumber and cotton, of cattle and buffalo — and in Texas yesterday is never far away. It is, after all, not too much more than 100 years ago that bandits plundered, Indians raided and Texas fought to be free — and to become the wealthy gem it is today.

Left These ranks of cattle graze on pasture land beneath the Davis Mountains.

Below These cattle seem to be taking the opportunity for cautious examination of horse and rider while both relax in the stockyard.

Right This timeless country store shows that some faces of Texas have hardly changed over the years.

Below The Indians have retained their old skills of ornamental beadwork, weaving and crafts. There were originally several tribes in Texas, ranging from peaceful farmers to the cannibalistic Karankawas.

Above This French trading post at Beaumont dates back to 1845 and is a wonderful example of the craft of those early builders of log cabins.

Left After a hard day on the range, a mug of hot coffee and a meal cooked over an open fire is more than welcome.

Above At Permian Basin, old pieces of drilling
equipment mirror the colors of the rich and
fertile soil of Texas.

Right The Permian Basin Petroleum Museum
at Midlands has on display antiquated
machinery that must once have seemed very
sophisticated to the cowpoke.

Above The search for new oil wells goes on unceasingly. Strange to think that oil was once considered a nuisance, as it polluted precious water holes.

Left Perhaps one day this oil refinery currently under construction will be displayed in a museum.

Facing page and above The lumber industry is big in Texas, too. In a state with so many natural resources, people live high on the hog.

Left This bewildering maze of pipes is in fact a natural gas refinery, pumping yet more energy to keep industry on the move.

Above Star-shaped orange blossom in the Lone Star State. Texas is studded with groves of citrus fruit.

Right All the sun in Texas seems to have gone into this luscious looking crop.

Facing page Cotton; a precious crop in times past, now less so due to the growth of synthetic products – but still picturesque to look at and evocative of the days when the boll weevil could take away a man's livelihood.

CHAPTER 3

Famous Cities

For many, the biggest and the best is "The Big D" — Dallas. Once it was a mere trading post. Today, in combination with neighboring Fort Worth, it claims the world's largest airport, probably more Cadillacs per capita than any place outside the Arab world, and wealth beyond measure. For all that, the city is rather conservative.

Dallas folk don't like to talk about the assassination of President Kennedy, yet the Texas Book Depository has become the city's most photographed site. From here Lee Harvey Oswald took his fatal aim.

In honor of the assassinated president, Dallas dedicated John F. Kennedy Memorial Plaza, slightly away from the city's bustle, and erected a towering cenotaph. In the John F. Kennedy Museum, a multimedia presentation gives particular emphasis to those final hours.

To see Dallas as it is today, take the elevator to the observation terrace at the First National Bank and enjoy a panoramic view from the fiftieth floor. Or indulge in a cocktail or meal in the revolving sky-high restaurant at Reunion Tower, which also has an observation deck.

To see Dallas as it used to be, head for City Park, where restored Victorian houses, railroad depots and pioneer log cabins give a glimpse into the past. The city's founder, John Neely Bryan, built his cabin in 1841 — it's on view across from the Kennedy Memorial. For the more down-to-earth, go to Farmers Market where farmers bring their fresh produce to sell. There's always a colorful character or two to be seen there.

The best time to visit Fair Park is in October, during the annual State Fair, but it's a permanent exhibition with various museums, attractions and restaurants, as well as being home to the Cotton Bowl stadium and Fair Park Coliseum. The Museum of Natural History is here,

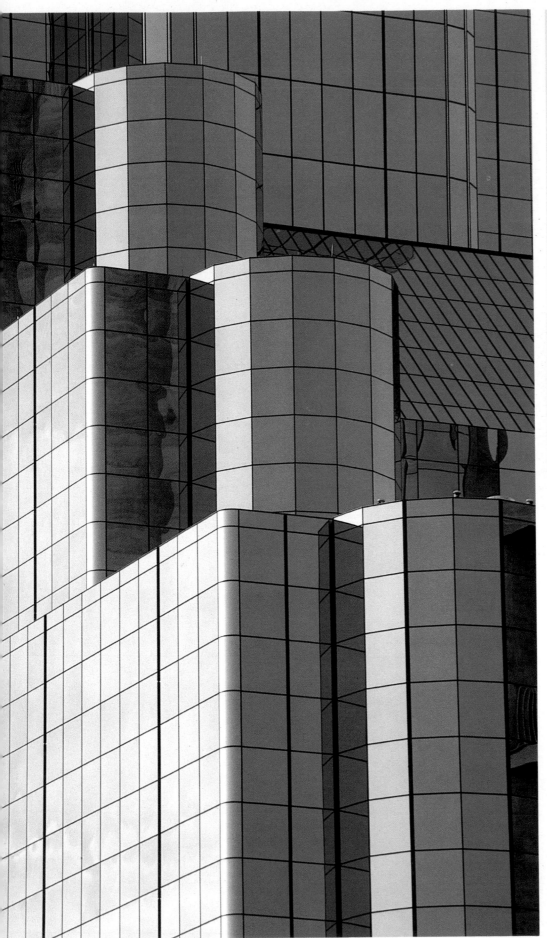

containing within its limestone walls a display of Southwest flora and fauna. Until it moves to its new home, the Museum of Fine Arts is also located here. So is the Age of Steam Railroad Museum, with its historical collection covering the years 1900 to 1950. Near the Aquarium is the Garden Center, showing continuous horticultural exhibits. And in the Health & Science Museum you'll find fascinating transparent models of a man and a woman — that talk!

All the fun of the fair is to be found along the Midway, lined with rides and food stands. The carnival activity is at its most frenetic during the State Fair but there's also fun to be had on weekends. At one end of the Midway stands the Hall of State, built in 1936 to commemorate the Centennial of Texas Independence.

Since Dallas is a major clothing manufacturing and design center, fashion shops are numerous. But no one store is more fashionable than Neiman Marcus, surprisingly unpretentious from the outside and astonishingly expensive on the inside. Many of the exotic goods for which it is renowned are listed in the store's famous Christmas catalog.

There is no one area for nightlife, which ranges from dinner theater to jazz and rock clubs. Many of the clubs require membership. Beef is quite naturally king on the restaurant scene, from hamburgers to "Texas fried steak" — a deep-fried, breaded cut of steak — but Dallas is cosmopolitan enough to have European, Oriental and Mexican restaurants, too. Culturally, the Music Hall is the place for concerts — home to the Dallas Symphony Orchestra and setting for summer musicals, as well as the Dallas Civic Opera. In the Dallas Theater Center, year-round performances range from Shakespeare to the avant-garde.

For the kids, there's always a visit to the Zoo or to L.B. Houston Park, a wildlife area. The International Wildlife Park at Arlington, further out of Dallas, is the only preserve of its kind in the Southwest. In the same location is Six Flags over Texas, a themed amusement park, and the Southwestern Wax Museum.

Fort Worth tends to be more "Western" than its neighbor. Much of its heritage is recaptured in the Historic Stockyards area on the northside where frontier-style cafés and shops line its boardwalks. Restored

1850 log cabins are clustered at Log Cabin Village and Fort Worth has several notable museums of its own.

Gleaming Houston rises mirage-like from the Texas prairie in a splendid array of smoked and bronzed skyscrapers. Its titles — Oil Center of the Nation, Space City USA, Banking Capital of the Southwest — have turned it from "Cowtown" to "The Sunbelt's Golden Buckle". It's young and brash, bright and racy, gathering many continentals in its midst.

To see Houston as it is, take a revolve around the Spindletop of the Hyatt Regency Hotel. To see Houston as it was, visit Sam Houston Park with its restored nineteenth century shops and homes. It adjoins the Civic Center, where there are other open-air niches: Tranquility Park, commemorating the Moon Landing; Herman Square, in front of City Hall, and Jones Plaza, the raised tree-lined area in front of Jones Hall for the Performing Arts. Then there's Old Market Square, which encloses an Indian trading post and an inn where General Sam Houston once stayed.

Most of the money is to be found in the River Oaks section of town, the green-

Above The Texas School Book Depository, from where Lee Harvey Oswald fired the bullet that killed President Kennedy and ended an era on November 22, 1963.

Far left and center The Reunion Tower tells the story as to how modern and innovative Dallas has become. It has a glass elevator which goes to an observation deck 50 stories up for a grand view over the city.

belted home of the rich. Here are palatial mansions and big estates. Most of the fun is to be found on Westheimer — the International Strip as it's called. This lively neighborhood is noted for its offbeat boutiques, its discos and folk clubs, its unusual restaurants and little piano bars.

In town there are underground shop-lined walkways, but the Galleria Mall, away from downtown, is probably the most elegant. This complex boasts its own hotel, skating rink, tennis courts and medical center, plus a host of elegant department and specialty stores.

Nouveau riche it might be, but Houston still has its cultural side. There are many theaters and dinner theaters. Performances are given outdoors in summer at the Miller Theater in Herman Park and in the Music Hall, while Jones Hall for the Performing Arts is home to the city's Symphony Orchestra, Ballet and Grand Opera companies. Museums include the Natural Science, the largest of its kind in the

Southwest, and the Fine Arts, which houses interesting Indian art and a modern sculpture garden.

Like Dallas and Fort Worth, Houston loves sports and what could be better than a visit to the Astrodome, some six miles from the city center. This giant, domed stadium, with its suitably enormous scoreboard, can hold 66000 spectators. Next door is Astroworld, a theme park, which offers everything from performing dolphins to water-skiing spectaculars; rides guaranteed to make you scream and a host of other amusements.

The NASA Lyndon B. Johnson Space Center training ground for astronauts and the monitoring center for NASA manned space flights is located 25 miles to the southeast. Films, exhibits and a tour of the Mission Control Center are all available.

Those willing to travel out of town (and in Houston a car is a necessity anyway), can discover the San Jacinto Battleground park. A 570-foot monument marks the spot

Center and above These nineteenth century buildings are to be found in the Old City Park in Dallas. This 12-acre site depicts Texas in the years 1840 through 1910 and contains residential houses, a railroad depot, a general store and a doctor's surgery.

Left The buildings in Pioneer Square make odd neighbors but that is what makes Dallas such an exciting city.

Far left The Galleria is one of the most fashionable shopping centers in Dallas, containing Tiffany's, Saks and Marshall Field, as well as up to the minute leisure facilities.

where Sam Houston defeated Mexican General Santa Anna. The park's museum reveals everything you ever wanted to know about Texas history and shows off the battleship *Texas*, berthed on the Houston Ship Channel. Sightseeing tours down the channel, aboard the *Sam Houston*, can be reserved.

It's a 50-mile trip to the nearest beach resort — Galveston, on the Gulf of Mexico. This city is an island sandbar linked by causeway to the mainland. Water sports of all kinds are good here and the island has its own golf courses and tennis clubs. In the restored Strand area, you'll find a number of interesting cafés, craft shops and art galleries. In the restored "Silk Stocking District" are a number of palatial residences including the Walter Gresham Home, nicknamed "The Bishop's Palace", and once the setting for many an elaborate party. These renovated districts, together with the outdoor historical drama *The Lone Star* (staged at Galveston State Park), help demonstrate the fact that the city was a Southwest cultural and commercial emporium at the turn of the century. It no longer tries to be "Sin City of the Texas Gulf Coast", as it was called in the 1940s, but it's still a lively place.

Ranches and reservations dot the state of Texas. Thirty miles from Houston there's Western action for tourists at Simonton's Round-up Rodeo. Yes, there are cowboys aplenty, western dancing (true Texans do *not* take their stetsons off!) and the opportunity to enjoy a barbeque. The state's largest Indian reservation is the Alabama-Courshatta in Livingston (75 miles from Houston). Visitors are welcomed to tour the Big Thicket Swamp, watch tribal dances and purchase crafts.

Above Mirror images in a skyscraper in Houston must be making life difficult for the window cleaner!

Above left This statue of Robert E. Lee near Turtle Creek commemorates one of America's most famous soldiers.

Left Houston is a city of opportunity and industry, the skyline constantly changing with new buildings thrusting up. These freeways carry many a hopeful new resident looking for a brand new life.

Right Samuel Houston, the first president of the Republic of Texas, was in fact a Virginian, and was governor of Tennessee until his bride left him after their honeymoon. The scandal sent him to Oklahoma Territory, from whence he moved to Texas three years later.

Right The Astrodome, home of the Houston Oilers and the Houston Astros baseball team. Quite often it's standing room only in this huge arena. It opened in 1965, the first domed stadium larger than an outdoor football field.

Below Texans love a splash – you couldn't possibly fail to notice the scoreboard!

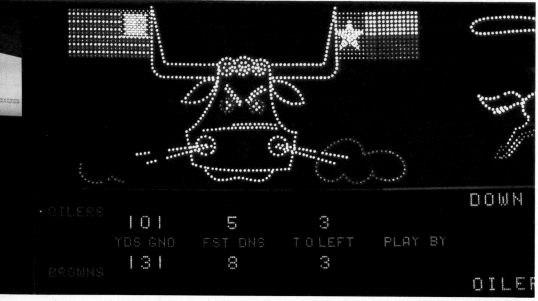

Below Texas is not all oilwells and cattle – there is a thriving cultural scene as well. The Houston Symphony Orchestra, seen here, is of international renown.

Above and far left In April the Westheimer Art Fair brings the crowds to enjoy art and entertainment in the streets.

Right Houston has many faces – this scene downtown is, remember, in the same city as the Astrodome.

Below You can take a 90-minute tour of the Port of Houston on the *Sam Houston.* Be prepared to be patient, though – there is a three-month reservation wait!

Left Texan architecture has a wonderful way of combining the ultra-modern with flowing shapes and luxuriant greenery.

Below Sam Houston Park has several nineteenth century houses and a church, although only one is on its original site – the Kellum-Noble House, which dates from 1847 and is the oldest brick house in the city.

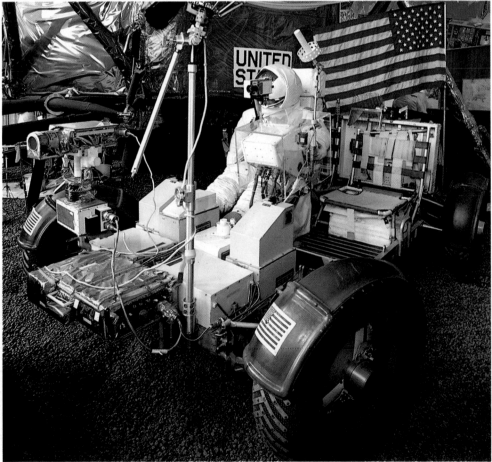

Houston's most famous feature – the NASA/
Lyndon B. Johnson Space Center. One of the
technological wonders of the world, it holds a
perennial fascination for thousands of visitors
who can go on guided tours of Mission Control
Center and the Space Environment Simulation
Laboratory. It's an unforgettable experience.

Above Galveston was once the major city in Texas, and at the same time, the Strand was known as the Wall Street of the South. These fine old iron front buildings have been recently restored and redecorated.

Right Sealy Street in Galveston has graceful and opulent houses. The historic area of Galveston is remarkable for the beauty and charm of its old buildings.

Left The Bishop's Palace on Broadway dates from 1893. In the terrible storm of 1900 which destroyed much of Galveston it provided shelter for many who found themselves suddenly homeless. It has belonged to the Catholic Church since 1933, but is open to anyone who wishes to admire its splendor.

Below Although Galveston fell prey in the past to violent storms and tidal waves, a seventeen-foot sea wall running for ten miles means that beach homes are now safe to live in.

Above The *Elissa* is the third-oldest merchant ship on the water. She was built in Scotland in 1877, and docked at Galveston, laden with cargo, in 1883. After a long career, during which she was even used as a smuggling ship, she was discovered in a sorry state in Greece by the Galveston Historical Foundation. Now completely restored, she is her former proud self.

Right Under Texas laws, all beaches are open to the public. Galveston Island has 32 miles of beachfront, with magnificent surfing.

Above Galveston's early civic importance had more than a little to do with its fine harbor, which can accommodate over a hundred ships at once.

Left Galveston is a gourmet's paradise, and this is reflected in the restaurants, where you can sample some of the finest seafood and salads in the world.

CHAPTER 4

The Spanish-Mexican Influence

When the Spanish set sail and arrived in America, Texas was part of the land under their rule from 1519 to 1685. These were times which saw many power struggles; next came the French but Spain took over the reins once more between 1719 and 1821. Texas was part of newly-independent Mexico from 1821 to 1836, until revolution won it its independence.

It's not surprising that, in some places, Spanish and Mexican influences linger on, and nowhere more so than in beautiful San Antonio. Here, a heroic stand was taken by Texan troops against the Mexican Army at a frontier fort and mission. It was, of course, at The Alamo, now a museum. There were 188 Texan heroes including William Travis, Jim Bowie and Davy Crockett, who made their stand against General Santa Anna and 5000 men. Though they all went down fighting, The Alamo is long remembered.

San Antonio was established in 1718 by the Spanish who came here to convert the Indians and it still boasts lovely adobe buildings. The first residential area was La Villita which, thanks to clever restoration, looks much the same now as it did 250 or so years ago. But the homes which once housed early settlers today house artisans practicing old crafts like glass-blowing, weaving and dollmaking. Among the buildings to look for are the Cos House, built in 1835, where General Cos, commander of the Mexican forces, surrendered to the Texans; also the Old San Antonio Museum.

The only remaining Spanish colonial mansion in Texas is the Spanish Governor's Palace, built in 1749 when the state was a Spanish province. Now restored, it is a National Historical Landmark. El Mercado is an original marketplace which has been renovated to retain its Spanish buildings. Nowadays, it's Mexican merchants who offer tempting handicrafts here.

While The Alamo was the first of five

missions established under Spanish rule, it is not the only one in existence along the well-marked Mission Trail starting at the southern tip of the city. The most famous is Mission San Jose, called the "Queen of Missions". Established in 1720, the original parish church features "Rosa's Window", an impressive stone carving, and is a National Historic Site. Mission Concepción is the oldest unrestored mission in the country, also a National Historical Landmark. Notable for its fine frescoes, Mission San Francisco de la Espada, established in 1720, is still active as a Catholic church.

Pioneers from many countries were drawn to San Antonio and today a number of ethnic groups remain. The biggest group is the Mexican Americans, making the city largely bilingual and a blend of cultures. The former German quarter is in the King William area, where the German community lived in splendor during the nineteenth century. More than 80 homes have been restored here, including Steves Homestead, one such fashionable residence of the 1870s.

The ethnic mix provides San Antonio with a choice of restaurants ranging from Polish to Chinese, though it is still the Mexican spots, where mariachis play, that

Far left Mission San José is the largest and most sumptuous mission, with elaborate carvings. The missions were also used as granaries, schools and forts.

Below left Nowhere in San Antonio is the Spanish influence more evident than in the Catholic missions. Mission Concepción was built in 1731 and is the oldest Texan mission in its original state.

Left Who has not heard of Davy Crockett? He died here at the Alamo, when 188 gallant Texans tried vainly to repel a Mexican army of 5000. Although they lost the battle, they made the Alamo an American legend.

Below San Antonio has honored its heroes – Davy Crockett is immortalized in this memorial, complete with his famous hat.

TRAVIS   CROCKETT

KERR · GEORGE C. KIMBLE · WILLIAM P. KING · JOHN G. KING · WILLIAM IRVINE LEWIS · WILLIAM J. LIGHTFOOT · JONATHAN
McKINNEY · ELIEL MELTON · THOMAS R. MILLER · WILLIAM MILLS · ISAAC MILLSAPS · EDWARD F. MITCHASSON · EDW
PAGAN · CHRISTOPHER A. PARKER · JUAN ANTONIO PADILLO · WILLIAM PARKS · RICHARDSON PERRY · AMOS POLLARI
NS · ANDREW H. SMITH · CHARLES S. SMITH · JOSHUA G. SMITH · WILLIAM H. SMITH · RICHARD STARR · JOHN W. S
N M. THRUSTON · BURKE TRAMMEL · WILLIAM BARRET TRAVIS · GEORGE W. TUMLINSON · ASA WALKER · JACOB WAL

give San Antonio its special atmosphere. This is especially true on the Paseo del Rio, the walkway along the horseshoe bend of the San Antonio River. The river walk, 20 feet below street level, is reached by steps and is lined with hotels, cafés and gift shops set amid tropical foliage.

The river winds through Brackenridge Park where there are several tourist attractions. A miniature railway will appeal to the children while riders can hire horses to trot along the park's bridle paths. The decorative Sunken Gardens feature winding walkways around pools brimming with water lilies, while the free Sky Ride gives a panoramic view of the park and nearby Fort Sam Houston. Brackenridge is also the home of San Antonio's zoo.

Talking of animals, circus fans will enjoy the Hertzberg Circus Collection, which traces circus development from its English origins to American three-ring extravaganzas. The Buckhorn Hall of Horns, an old-time saloon now the property of the Lone Star Brewing Company, features horned game trophies.

When San Antonio marked its 250th birthday in 1968, it hosted the World's Fair. Hemis Fair Plaza is the legacy, with the best city viewing point atop the Tower of the Americas. Also here is the Institute of Texan Cultures, which examines the ethnic groups who contributed to Texas' history, and a

Left The Spanish Governor's Palace was built in 1749 and was the residence of the Spanish governors who ruled Texas.

Far left and below This charming simple chapel with its ancient timber is in the Spanish Governor's Palace. Outside is a cool leafy garden – a perfect place for a quiet moment.

multimedia presentation of Texas.

El Paso, on the Rio Grande, is very Mexican. It is, after all, just across the border from Juarez. It was a Spaniard who first explored the region in 1536, but the earliest settlement, established in 1598, was destroyed by Indians. The Spanish tried again in 1659 and this settlement later became Juarez. By 1827, the El Paso area was known as the Ponce de Leon Ranch, and the town, Franklin. When the latter became US territory after the Mexican War, it was renamed El Paso for the nearby pass through the mountains — El Paso del Norte.

El Paso boomed when the railroads arrived in the 1880s. Those were the days of gamblers and gangsters like John Wesley Hardin, perhaps the fastest and deadliest gun in the west, and that notorious bandit, Pancho Villa. Billy the Kid, Bat Masterson and Pat Garrett shot their way up here also.

Today, this border city doesn't stand for lawlessness, but visitors can take a trip back in time by going to La Villita whose old town shopping village includes several restored heritage homes which have been turned into boutiques and galleries. Walk through the quarter's brick archway and you'll be in the exact spot where Luz Villa, Pancho's favorite wife, once had her home. Pancho Villa may have had a reputation as an outlaw but he also had one as a lover!

La Villita is not the only reminder of the past. The Magoffin Homestead is an abode hacienda, built in 1875 and now a museum. It may be dwarfed by the downtown skyscrapers, but its sun-dried brick remains stout — four feet thick in fact. Wood used in the home was all handhewn and brought by wagons from Mescalero in the mountains around 100 miles to the north. Some of the furnishings on view date from the time of the original owner.

California's missions may be well known but those in El Paso's Lower Valley are older. Nuestra Señora del Carmen, for example, was established in 1681 for the Tigua Indians. Nuestra Señora de la Concepción del Socorro was a pueblo and mission complex established by refugees from what is now New Mexico after the Pueblo Revolt in 1681. And the San Elizario Presidio Chapel, founded in 1777 to serve Spanish military personnel, is still in daily use.

One of El Paso's main attractions is the Tigua Indian Reservation on the eastern edge of the city. The Tiguas are one of two recognized Texas Indian tribes who operate

Right The Old Train Station in San Antonio shows the Spanish influence in its graceful balustrades and high domed roof.

Left Fort Sam Houston was where Mamie and Ike Eisenhower met each other, and they subsequently lived here. An earlier inhabitant was Geronimo, who was held captive in the quadrangle.

Below San Antonio's river makes up in charm for what it lacks in size. Narrow and looping, in places it is hardly navigable, but the River Walk is crammed with cafés, shops and ethnic restaurants, making the river a truly lively place to stroll beside.

a living pueblo within city limits. They came to Texas to flee the Pueblo Revolt, settling in a place they called Ysleta del Sur, where they built their own mission. Nowadays, young Tiguas learn both the customs of their forefathers and the skills of the modern world and tourists are welcomed to eat in their restaurants, see their crafts and watch ceremonial dances.

Another must is a ride on the aerial tramway for a view of two nations. You'll be whisked to the top of the mountains in minutes to look out over Chihuahua, Texas and New Mexico. To the east are the Hueco and Guadalupe Mountains; to the north, the Organ Mountains and, in the distance, New Mexico's White Sands. Mexico rolls south, with the Florida Mountains in view to the west.

At the Fort Bliss Replica Museum there's a reminder of how the US Army has stood guard over the frontiers during America's

growth. The building is a reproduction of how Fort Bliss looked in 1854 and on the grounds surrounding it are wagons and weapons, from Gatling guns to missiles.

On a mountain peak about three miles west of El Paso stands a silent guardian — Cristo Rey. The shrine, sculpted out of white stone, can be seen from most parts of the valley and city. Another memorial is the Chamizal, a tribute to international cooperation. For centuries, the Rio Grande has changed its course between the sister cities of El Paso and Juarez, resulting in controversy as to who owned which land. In 1893, Mexico laid claim to the Chamizal tract and the US made counterclaims. Finally, in 1963, a treaty was signed and efforts were made to prevent future boundary changes. A part of the land acquired from Mexico was given up for the memorial, which includes a museum where tapestries and artworks are displayed. Across the Rio Grande, Mexico has established a companion commemorative park.

El Paso is surrounded by natural wonders. It's a city which loves sports and has an amphitheater in McKelligon Canyon for outdoor productions. A new themed amusement park, Magic Landing, is aimed at providing entertainment for all the family with computerized and automated rides, plenty of shops and eating places, game arcades and a youngsters' playground.

But no visitor to El Paso would miss crossing the border to Juarez itself. No special papers are needed for a stay of less than 72 hours and three bridges allow entry by foot, taxi or sightseeing bus. Drivers generally use the Cordova Bridge at Chamizal. Everyone comes to shop for onyx and leather goods, paper flowers, silver, tin and pottery. Everyone comes to sip a margarita or two, dip into guacamole and listen to a mariachi tune.

Traditionally, the shopping area is Juarez Avenue but the government-built PRONAF, near the Cordova crossing, is a showcase for the best of Mexican arts and crafts. Spices and herbs permeate the air in the City Market and on Sundays the plaza around the Benito Juarez Monument is filled with street entertainers. And on Sundays, too, in season, a charreada (Mexican rodeo) takes place in the Lopez Mateos Charro Arena.

The two cities' history is so interlinked that they are almost as one, but they're not the only sister Tex-Mex cities. Brownsville/ Matamoros, McAllen/Reynosa, Laredo/ Nuevo Laredo are among the predominant ones. All are so bilingual that "Buenos dias" is heard as often as "Howdy".

The Mexican vaqueros or charros — those magnificent horsemen — were indeed the forerunners of the Texas

Above Rodeo Mexican-style. The flavor may be a little different, but the skills are the same.

Left This simple and beautiful piece of architecture at the Socorro Mission, built in 1681, is typical of the Hispanic style of El Paso.

Facing page above and below The Lone Star Brewery is the home of the beer trucks, and of exhibits of stuffed animals. These deer are to be found in the Buckhorn Hall of Horns: the old Buckhorn Saloon and O. Henry's house are also on the site.

cowboys. It was they who helped to tame the herds of wild longhorns on the open south Texas range. It was they who taught Texans their riding skills and it was they who brought the leather chaps, bandannas, spurs, lariats, boots and broad-brimmed sombreros with them from across the border.

As mentioned earlier, this Tex-Mex flavor is due to the fact that Mexico gained independence from Spain in 1821 and acquired what was to become Texas. Colonization of the enormous area was encouraged using the same system as Spain. Land agents from the US and Mexico received large grants of cheap land for themselves and the settlers who followed. By 1836 when the Texians (as they called themselves then) declared their independence, the population had multiplied by seven in just 15 years.

Above These adobe buildings show the pueblo style of architecture. Some adobe walls are four feet thick.

Right This lady looks to be doing a lively trade with her pueblo jewelry.

Above A Texan-style barbecue with Mexican-style cabaret!

Left Spanish-American politics are often expressed in art. This mural in Austin is painted on plywood.

CHAPTER 5

Naturally Big Is Beautiful

Sands and grasslands that shimmer in the sun stretch for over 100 miles along the south coast of Texas that comprises Padre Island, longest of the lean Gulf isles. Here, resorts share land with nature's best. Actually, Padre Island (named for Padre Nicholas Bali, who received it through a Spanish land grant) is two islands separated by a narrow sea channel.

Most of the developed holiday areas are to the south near Brownsville, while much of the north forms National Seashore Park where breeze-swept dunes are unblemished by towns and villages and only flocks of birds cloud the sky. In the 80-mile park, you can camp, fish, swim and beachcomb in peace. The sand probably still hides Spanish gold but the fierce Karankawa Indians are no longer here.

Beaches up and down Padre, including Malaquite, are open to overnight guests. South of Malaquite, the popular Grasslands Trail offers a well-marked walk through waving grasses and shifting dunes. For more comfortable accommodation, choose Port Aransas or Corpus Christi as a base. Corpus Christi's harbor is filled with pleasure boats and boasts a kind climate the year round, while Port Aransas not only gives direct access to the Seashore Park but has its own wildlife refuge plus 18 miles of sparkling white beach.

The pale gold sands of the south Padre are lined with hotels and motels and Isla Blanca Park is ideal for a day's outing. Across the Laguna Madre (connected by causeway), Port Isobel offers a haven for the city-weary. It has been a resort since the mid 1800s and nowadays offers deluxe accommodation close by.

But enough of beaches — there is so much more. Texas has 90 state parks and two national ones. The Guadalupe Mountains National Park on the northwestern border with New Mexico

Above The outgoing tide leaves pools of liquid silver on the Texas shoreline. In the background, the low hump of Padre Island.

may be a relatively new one but it encompasses four of the state's highest peaks including the highest of all — Guadalupe Peak, a dominant 8751 feet tall. Sections of the park are forested, others are meadows and some parts plunge into deep canyons. McKittrick Canyon is the only one accessible by car but backpackers and hikers have their choice. Retaining the natural unspoiled element has meant limited accommodation: you can camp around Dog Canyon and Pine Springs but the nearest hotel is in White's City, 35 miles away in New Mexico.

Big Bend National Park is far larger — 900 000 acres of southwest Texas that are memorable though remote. It's a park of scenic contrasts encompassing miles and miles of deserts, the towering Chisos Mountains, a multitude of volcanic formations and the sheer canyons of the Rio Grande.

Big Bend is an awe-inspiring place; the area was once an ocean and, in pre-historic times, dinosaurs walked here and the giant pterodactyl flew over it. It's so vast that a first call must be made at the park's headquarters at Panther Junction. From here there are driving tours, saddle horse trips, hiking routes and rafting excursions. Accommodation is limited to campsites and a few cabins and lodges.

The largest state park is Palo Duro Canyon south of Amarillo in the middle of the western Panhandle. Over 15 000 acres surround the magnificent canyon where the Red River has carved spires and pinnacles and canyon walls rise a thousand feet. This was the scene of the last great Indian battle in 1874, between the US Cavalry and the Comanches, but the site also has an amphitheater used in summer for dramatic musical presentations. The park offers horseback riding, hiking trails and camping.

Much of Texas is about natural phenomena like the wind-sculptured sand dunes of Monahans Sandhills State Park. It looks like the Sahara and proved as much

Above Most of the shoreline of Padre Island is a National Seashore – a paradise for both the beachcomber and the birdwatcher.

Left A snowy egret presenting a dramatic silhouette at dawn.

of an obstacle to the early pioneers in their wagon trains, especially since the Indians knew it better and often camped here. Today, it's no problem to camp or picnic or take a sand-buggy ride over the dunes and the park has a modern museum and interpretive center.

East Texas is the region for many of the state's forests and lakes. There are four national forests of which Angelina is the smallest. Recreational areas here can be found at Boykin Springs; Letney and Townsend, both on Lake Sam Rayburn; Harvey Creek; Caney Creek; Sandy Creek and Bouton Lake. In Davy Crockett National Forest, recreational centers are at Ratcliff Lake, Neches Bluff, Kickapoo and Big Slough Canoe Trail. Visitors to Sam Houston National Forest should make for Double Lake, Stubblefield Lake, Big Creek Scenic Area, Scott's Ridge or Lone Star Hiking Trail. And in the largest forest, Sabine, recreational bases are located at Boles Field, Indian Mounds, Lakeview, Ragtown, Red Hills Lake and Willow Oak.

Texas' four state forests — Fairchild, Jones, Kirby and Siecke — are all wildlife

refuges so no hunting is allowed and fishing only in designated areas. All feature a self-guided nature trail and areas for picnicking and swimming.

As naturally beautiful as all these places are, Texas makes full use of its splendid geography in another way — excursions with an "Old West" theme. A day out at a ranch may very well mean traveling by horse-drawn wagon to some beauty spot, through prairies where buffalo once roamed in their hundreds. Breakfast out of doors will mean Texan-sized helpings of eggs and sausage accompanied by sourdough biscuits baked over an open campfire. There may well be demonstrations of roping, branding and other cowboy activities.

Eating trail dust, as they say, is really quite easy. Just join the real cowboys during the

Above In the Guadalupe Mountains National Park you will find deer and elk in the alpine meadows, wonderful walking trails, and the highest peak in Texas.

Left Leafy detail of a creosote bush growing in Guadalupe National Park.

Facing page Lush greenery in Guadalupe National Park contrasts with the stern grey bulk of the mountain behind.

Facing page far left El Capitan in Guadalupe Mountains National Park; sunrise illuminates its sheer craggy sides and lower flanks of scree.

annual spring Longhorn Trail Drive at the
Y.O. Ranch near Kerrville. This is one of the
largest of the state's ranches open to the
public and the weekend trail drive allows
you to sample the real thing.

Similarly, Indian Cliffs Ranch (not far from
El Paso) features the "cowboy experience".
A desert trail leads to Fort Misery, an
authentic re-creation of a desert outpost
that looks as if it's in the middle of nowhere
but is actually not far from the ranch
headquarters. Steak cookouts, cowboy
serenading and an overnight bedroll under
the stars or in the fort are the order of things.
But a touch of modernity the pioneers
wouldn't have known — real toilets!

Working ranches are scattered
throughout the state — the biggest spread

is the King Ranch, covering 800 000 acres of
south Texas. Most of the dude ranches are
located in the hill country around Bandera
and are often family run. Expect cabin-style
accommodation; huge meals and home-
spun entertainment. Plus as much riding as
your rear end will take.

Reconstructed private and military forts
are settings for Old West re-creations. Fort
Parker, for example, was the scene of a
Comanche attack in 1836 in which a
nine-year-old girl was captured by Indians
and was forced to live with them for 24
years, during which time she became the
mother of the last great Comanche chief,
Quanah Parker. The saga is retold at the fort
each May. Fort Davis, garrisoned from 1854
to 1891, was a rest stop for gold-seekers on
their way west. Echoes of the times are
heard hourly during the day as a military
retreat parade sounds across the deserted

Left and below Palo Duro Canyon State Park is the site of the last major battle with the Indians. The canyon itself is several miles long, and in places 800 feet deep. This underground home and lighthouse are just two of the historic sites to be seen.

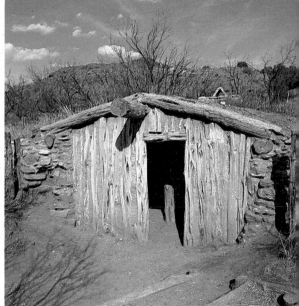

Left This bobcat is certainly a relation of the domestic tabby, but is one of the most ferocious members of the feline species. When this kitten is fully-grown it will be a creature to treat with considerable respect.

Facing page The fabled Rio Grande; a vital escape route for outlaws of the past. Nowadays the traffic is mainly in the other direction, with Mexicans seeking the good life across the border. Despite its name, it is in some places little more than a trickle of water.

Facing page far left These strange-looking holes in Big Bend National Park are, in fact, holes for grinding corn made by the Indians.

parade ground.

West of the Pecos there are ghost mining towns and vast volcanic deposits, a place where rock and mineral collectors could well come away with rich rewards — onyx and quartz, for example. Another famous mineral region is the Llano Uplift of central Texas where garnet and topaz can be found.

Such diverse terrain has colored Texas with a variety of flowers. In the eastern marshlands, pitcher plants trap insects. In western canyons rare red Mexican silenes grow. Morning glories brighten the Padre dunes and in the Lower Rio Grande Valley the boulevards are aflame with bougainvillea.

Wildlife, too, is abundant in Texas. Indeed, the state claims it has more varieties of birds than any other. Along the shoreline are huge flocks of gulls, pelicans, egrets and some of the world's few remaining whooping cranes, which winter at the Aransas National Wildlife Refuge.

Tropical birds home in on the Lower Rio Grande Valley, said to be the only place in America where such species as chachalacas and green jays may be observed. Kites and prairie chickens make their home in the Texas Panhandle, while the Muleshoe National Wildlife Refuge is a haven for thousands of wintering sandhill cranes. Eagles and canyon wrens head for west Texas and the Hill Country is the nesting place for rare golden-cheeked warblers. In the pine forests of east Texas, look out for Acadian flycatchers and the wood thrush.

Anyone seeking a rodeo won't have to look far. During the summer months, rodeos take place in almost all Texas counties. The big indoor rodeos and livestock shows, however, are on a circuit which starts in Fort Worth in late January, moves to San Antonio in early February, then onto Houston later in the month. What visitor could leave Texas without seeing one of these rip-roaring events?

If big is beautiful — Texas naturally has everything in abundance!

Above This patch-nosed snake in Big Bend National Park seems to have a benign expression – but probably most people wouldn't want to get within striking distance, just in case.

Above left Texas is, needless to say, wonderful riding country – but there are so many sporting facilities in the state that it is just a matter of deciding which you prefer.

Left The tumbleweed, vivid symbol of the rootless cowboy of the past who owned nothing but his horse and his saddle.

Facing page above Boot Canyon, Big Bend National Park. The park is over 708000 acres in size with plentiful and varied wildlife. You can find every sort of scenery from lush forest to arid desert. Surprisingly, it is one of the least-visited national parks in the USA.

Facing page below The cracked and dried up river bed of the Rio Grande, in late summer.

Things to see in Texas

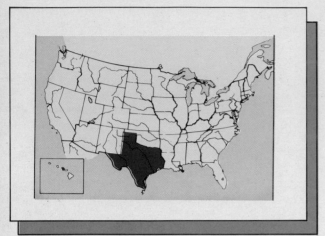

Ranching Heritage Center

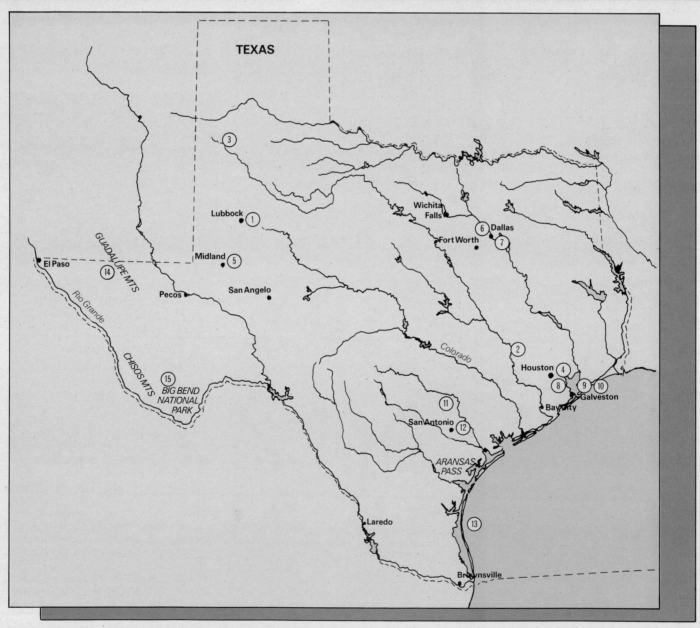

TEXAS

③

Lubbock ①

Wichita Falls

⑥ Dallas
Fort Worth ⑦

Midland ⑤

GUADALUPE MTS.

El Paso ⑭

Rio Grande

Pecos

San Angelo

Colorado

②

Houston ④

⑧ ⑨ ⑩
Galveston
Bay City

CHISOS MTS.

⑮
BIG BEND
NATIONAL
PARK

⑪

San Antonio ⑫

ARANSAS
PASS

Laredo

⑬

Brownsville

Guadalupe Mountains National Park

Lyndon B. Johnson Space Center

Old City Park

Elissa

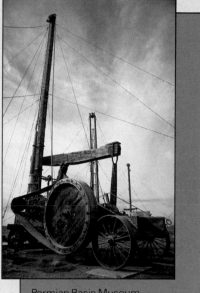
Permian Basin Museum

Bishop's Palace

1 The **Ranching Heritage Center** at Lubbock is a 12-acre site with 30 old ranches ranging from the most primitive to the most elegant. They have been collected from all over Texas, restored and furnished in period.

2 The **Texas State Capitol Building** in Austin dates from 1888, and is seven feet higher than the US Capitol. Its oak-shaded grounds are just right for a picnic.

3 The **Cadillac Ranch** at Amarillo is a startling sight – 10 Cadillacs nose-down in a wheatfield, demonstrating each tailfin design from 1949 through 1963.

4 The **Lyndon B. Johnson Space Center (NASA)** is the nerve center of America's space program. You can take guided tours to see lunar rock, training laboratories, simulated flight missions and all aspects of space technology

5 The **Permian Basin Museum** at Midland has examples of early oil machinery. Once the height of new technology, old oil drilling equipment now stands idle as a museum piece.

6 The **Reunion Tower** in Dallas is one of the most eye-catching examples of modern architecture. Its glass elevator rises to 50 stories, from where there is a magnificent view over the city.

7 The **Old City Park** in Dallas covers 12 acres and presents Texas from 1840 through 1910. It has authentic residential houses, a railroad depot, general store and doctor's surgery all from that period.

8 The **Astrodome** at Houston is home of the Houston Oilers and the Houston Astros baseball team. You can go there to watch some sport, or simply take a guided tour with multimedia presentation.

9 The **Bishop's Palace** on Broadway at Galveston was built in 1893 and has belonged to the Catholic Church since 1933. In the storm of 1900 which wrecked many Galveston houses it provided shelter for the homeless.

10 The **Elissa**, in Galveston harbor, is the third-oldest merchant ship in the water. She was built in Scotland in 1877 and after a long career was brought back to Galveston, where she had originally docked in 1883. She has been completely restored by the Galveston Historical Foundation.

11 The **Alamo** is legendary for every American. Davy Crockett died here in 1836 fighting the Mexican army against hopeless odds. He and the 187 others who died with him inspired the Texans to continue to struggle for independence.

12 **Mission San José**, in San Antonio, is the largest and most sumptuous of the Catholic missions. They were used for schools, granaries and forts as well as for religious purposes.

13 **Padre Island National Seashore** is an isolated paradise for the beachcomber and the birdwatcher. Padre Island is one of the longest islands in the US.

14 The **Guadalupe Mountains National Park** has alpine meadows, wonderful walking trails, and the highest peak in Texas.

15 **Big Bend National Park** contains widely varied and magnificent scenery, ranging from desert to lush forest. Over 708 000 acres in size, with a lot of wildlife, surprisingly it is one of the least-visited national parks in the US.

PICTURE CREDITS